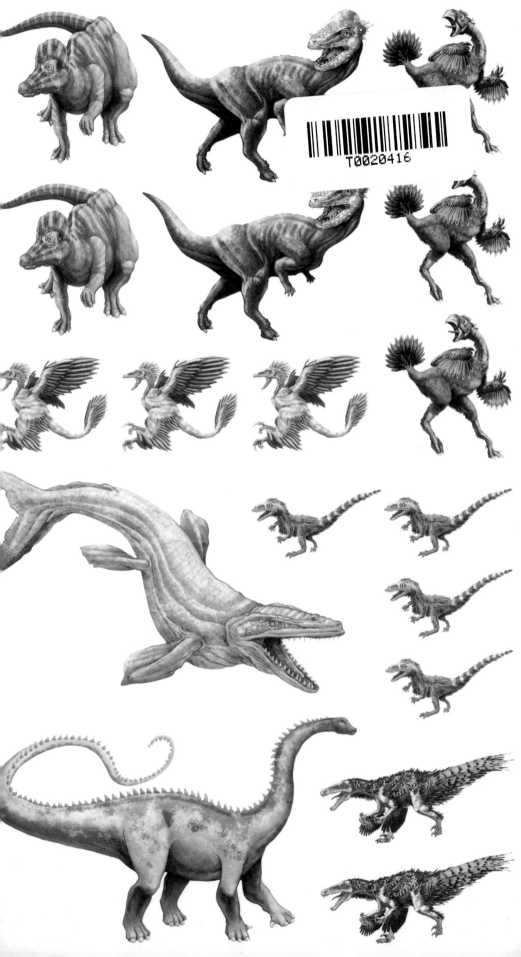

Caudipteryx

Pachycephalosaurus

Corythosaurus

Caudipteryx

Pachycephalosaurus

Corythosaurus

Caudipteryx

Microraptor

Microraptor

Microraptor

Sinosauropteryx

Sinosauropteryx

Mosasaurus

Sinosauropteryx

Sinosauropteryx

Velociraptor

Apatosaurus

Velociraptor

TO APPLY A

1 Cut out the tattoo and remove the plastic cover.

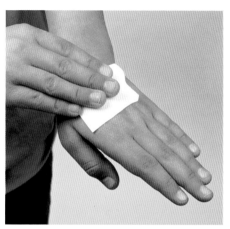

2 Stick the tattoo, picture-side down, onto clean, dry skin.

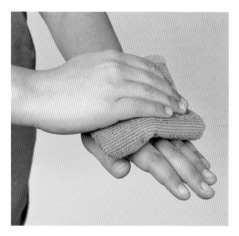

3 Place a wet cloth over the tattoo. Press down gently for about 30 seconds. Hold it still!

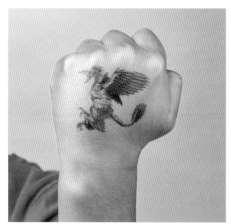

4 Gently slide off the paper backing. Do not touch until it's dry. Enjoy your bold body art!

TIP: To remove tattoos, dab with rubbing alcohol or baby oil. Wait 10 seconds, then rub gently. Apply more rubbing alcohol or baby oil repeatedly until removed.

◄ ALLOSAURUS
al-uh-SAWR-uhs

While growing, this huge meat-eater could gain more than 300 pounds per year. Full-grown *Allosaurus* were more than 30 feet long. It lived during the Late Jurassic period.

ANKYLOSAURUS ►
ain-kuh-loh-SAWR-uhs

Ankylosaurus weighed about 6 tons (around the size of a large elephant!) and ate plants. Its club-shaped tail was the same height as the knees of some of its predators, like *Tyrannosaurus*! It lived around 70 million years ago and was one of the last dinosaurs.

▼ APATOSAURUS
uh-pa-tuh-SAWR-uhs

This giant plant-eater could weigh almost 25 tons and was the length of two telephone poles! Its name comes from the Greek and means "deceptive lizard." *Apatosaurus* lived during the Late Jurassic period.

Brachiosaurus is closely related to Diplodocus and Apatosaurus! They are all in a group of dinosaurs called sauropods.

BRACHIOSAURUS›
brak-ee-oh-SAWR-uhs

Weighing in at 50 tons, *Brachiosaurus* is thought to be one of the largest dinosaurs! Its name means "arm reptile" since its front legs were much longer than its back legs. It lived during the Late Jurassic period.

▲CAUDIPTERYX
cah-DIP-tuhr-iks

This small dinosaur had long feathers like a bird, but its arms were too short for flying. It lived in what is now northeastern China during the Early Cretaceous period.

▲CORYTHOSAURUS
kuh-rith-uh-SAWR-uhs

This plant-eater lived in western North America during the Late Cretaceous period. It had a bony crest on the top of its head and its name means "helmet lizard" in Greek.

◄ DEINONYCHUS
dy-NON-ih-kuhs
In Greek, *Deinonychus* means "terrible claw." Walking on two legs, these dinosaurs had a 5-inch-long claw on each foot that could slice like a knife. The raptor in *Jurassic Park* was modeled after *Deinonychus*.

DILOPHOSAURUS►
dy-lahf-uh-SAWR-uhs
This sharp-toothed carnivore lived during the Early Jurassic period and was one of the earliest large meat-eaters. It had two thin crests on its head.

▲ DIPLODOCUS
duh-PLAH-dih-kuhs
From head to tail, *Diplodocus* was around 80 feet long. Its tail included nearly 80 vertebrae, making it the longest tail of any dinosaur. This plant-eater was lightweight for its size: it probably weighed only about 10 tons!

One of the most famous dinosaur skeletons is a *Diplodocus* named Dippy.

◄ EINIOSAURUS
y-nee-oh-SAWR-uhs

This plant-eater grew to around 15 feet long and weighed about 1½ tons. *Einiosaurus* lived in the Late Cretaceous period.

Paleontologists accidentally put together the first *Elasmosaurus* skeleton with the skull attached to the tail because they didn't believe its neck could be that long!

▲ ELASMOSAURUS
ih-las-muh-SAWR-uhs

The body of this marine reptile was more than 40 feet long. Its neck had more than 70 vertebrae, which is more than any other animal that lived during the Late Cretaceous period!

ICHTHYOVENATOR ►
ihk-thee-OH-vehn-ai-tuhr

This dinosaur's name means "fish hunter." It could grow to nearly 30 feet long (smaller than the similar *Spinosaurus*) and lived in Asia during the Early Cretaceous period.

◄ KENTROSAURUS
kehn-troh-SAWR-uhs

Appropriately, *Kentrosaurus* means "spiked reptile." Smaller than the more well-known *Stegosaurus*, this plant-eater grew to be only about 15 feet long. It lived in Africa during the Late Jurassic period.

Lambeosaurus ate plants by grinding their teeth together as cows do today!

▲ MICRORAPTOR
MY-kroh-rap-tuhr

This tiny meat-eater lived in what is now China during the Early Cretaceous period. It had long feathers on all four limbs and may have been able to glide between trees.

▲ LAMBEOSAURUS
lam-bee-oh-SAWR-uhs

This duck-billed dinosaur had many rows of teeth, called dental batteries, that were frequently replaced as they wore out. The hollow, hatchet-shaped crest at the top of its head was connected to its lungs.

◄ MOSASAURUS
moh-zuh-SAWR-uhs

This meat-eating marine reptile probably caught prey at the surface of the water. It lived during the Late Cretaceous period and could grow more than 40 feet long.

OVIRAPTOR ►
OH-vuh-rap-tuhr

This dinosaur got its name, meaning "egg hunter," because the first *Oviraptor* fossil was found with a nest of eggs, which paleontologists assumed the *Oviraptor* was eating. However, more recent discoveries show that *Oviraptors* sat on their own eggs to protect them — and ate plants, not eggs.

⌃PACHYCEPHALOSAURUS
pa-kee-sehf-uh-luh-SAWR-uhs
This dinosaur's name means "thick-headed reptile," and its domelike skull was often up to 10 inches thick. Palentologists used to think it was a plant-eater, but more recent studies on its teeth show that it probably ate meat.

⌃PARASAUROLOPHUS
pair-uh-sawr-AWL-uh-fuhs
Parasaurolophus may have used the hollow, 3-foot-long crest on top of its head to breathe and/or make noise. This plant-eating dinosaur lived throughout North America in the Late Cretaceous period.

⌃QUETZALCOATLUS
keht-suhl-kuh-WAHT-luhs
With a wingspan of around 36 feet, this pterosaur was one of the largest flying animals of all time. It ate meat, but there has been much debate over whether it was a scavenger or a hunter of small land animals.

⌃PTERANODON
tuh-RA-nuh-dahn
This pterosaur had a beak like a modern pelican that it used to snatch fish out of the water either while flying or swimming. *Pteranodon* lived in North America during the Late Cretaceous period.

Pterosaurs were covered with hair or down instead of feathers.

◤ SINOSAUROPTERYX

sy-noh-sawr-OP-tuhr-iks

This meat-eating dinosaur weighed only a little more than 1 pound and walked on two legs. Based on evidence in *Sinosauropteryx* fossils, scientists know that its tail had dark and light stripes.

◤ SPINOSAURUS

spy-nuh-SAWR-uhs

The largest of the meat-eating dinosaurs, *Spinosaurus* grew to more than 45 feet long! It lived in northern Africa, both on land and in the water, and may have used the sail on its back to attract mates.

STEGOSAURUS ►

steh-guh-SAWR-uhs

Found in Asia, Europe, and North America during the Late Jurassic period, this plant-eater is known for having one of the proportionally smallest brains of all the dinosaurs.

◤ STEGOSAURUS SKELETON

The plates on the back of *Stegosaurus* might have helped it regulate its body temperature, while the spike on its tail was used for defense. Paleontologist Othniel Charles Marsh found the first *Stegosaurus* bones in Colorado in 1877.

THERIZINOSAURUS▸

theh-ruh-zee-nuh-SAWR-uhs

This dinosaur's name means "scythe reptile," and it had the longest claws of any known dinosaur. Thought to eat plants, *Therizinosaurus* lived in Asia during the Late Cretaceous period.

◂TRICERATOPS

try-SEHR-uh-tahps

This plant-eater lived in North America during the Late Cretaceous period. It had a toothless beak at the end of its mouth, used for grabbing food or defending itself against predators.

TYRANNOSAURUS▸

tuh-ran-uh-SAWR-uhs

This large meat-eater with more than 50 teeth lived in western North America during the Late Cretaceous period. It walked on two legs and may have had some feathers. It is thought to have had the strongest bite of all the dinosaurs.

TYRANNOSAURUS SKELETON▸

Although *Tyrannosaurus* weighed more than 6 tons and was more than 40 feet long, its arms were only about the same size as a human's. The most complete *Tyrannosaurus* skeleton (85 percent) was discovered by Sue Hendrickson in Montana in 1990, and called Sue in her honor.

VELOCIRAPTOR►

vuh-LAH-suh-rap-tuhr

This predator weighed only around 30 pounds, which is much smaller than the velociraptor in the *Jurassic Park* movies. Its name means "swift hunter," and it lived in what is now China and Mongolia during the Late Cretaceous period.

Where Did Dinosaurs Live?

EUROPE
- Brachiosaurus
- Mosasaurus
- Stegosaurus

ASIA
- Caudipteryx
- Ichthyovenator
- Microraptor
- Oviraptor
- Sinosauropteryx
- Therizinosaurus
- Velociraptor

AFRICA
- Allosaurus
- Brachiosaurus
- Kentrosaurus
- Spinosaurus

AUSTRALIA
- Allosaurus

NORTH AMERICA
- Allosaurus
- Ankylosaurus
- Apatosaurus
- Brachiosaurus
- Corythosaurus
- Deinonychus
- Dilophosaurus
- Diplodocus
- Einiosaurus
- Elasmosaurus
- Lambeosaurus
- Mosasaurus
- Pachycephalosaurus
- Parasaurolophus
- Pteranodon
- Quetzalcoatlus
- Stegosaurus
- Triceratops
- Tyrannosaurus

How Big Were They?

APATOSAURUS
70 ft. (21 m)

DIPLODOCUS
80 ft. (24 m)

BRACHIOSAURUS
82 ft. (25 m)

TYRANNOSAURUS
46 ft. (14 m)

ELASMOSAURUS
43 ft. (13 m)

MOSASAURUS
40 ft. (12 m)

SPINOSAURUS
45 ft. (14 m)

CORYTHOSAURUS
33 ft. (10 m)

PARASAUROLOPHUS
36 ft. (11 m)

ALLOSAURUS
30 ft. (9 m)

THERIZINOSAURUS
33 ft. (10 m)

QUETZALCOATLUS
36 ft. (11 m)

ANKYLOSAURUS
33 ft. (10 m)

ICHTHYOVENATOR
30 ft. (9 m)

PTERANODON
23 ft. (7 m)

TRICERATOPS
30 ft. (9 m)

STEGOSAURUS
30 ft. (9 m)

LAMBEOSAURUS
30 ft. (9 m)

DILOPHOSAURUS
20 ft. (6 m)

PACHYCEPHALOSAURUS
15 ft. (5 m)

DEINONYCHUS
8 ft. (2 m)

EINIOSAURUS
15 ft. (5 m)

KENTROSAURUS
15 ft. (5 m)

CAUDIPTERYX
3 ft. (1 m)

SINOSAUROPTERYX
3 ft. (1 m)

MICRORAPTOR
3 ft. (1 m)

VELOCIRAPTOR
7 ft. (2 m)

OVIRAPTOR
7 ft. (2 m)